P9-ARD-404

THE PRESIDENCY AND
NATIONAL SECURITY POLICY

PROCEEDINGS SERIES:

Volume I – The White House: Organization and Operations

Volume II – The Presidency of the 1970s

Volume III – Organizing and Staffing the Presidency

Volume IV – The Presidency and Information Policy

Volume V – The Presidency and National Security Policy